MW01356091

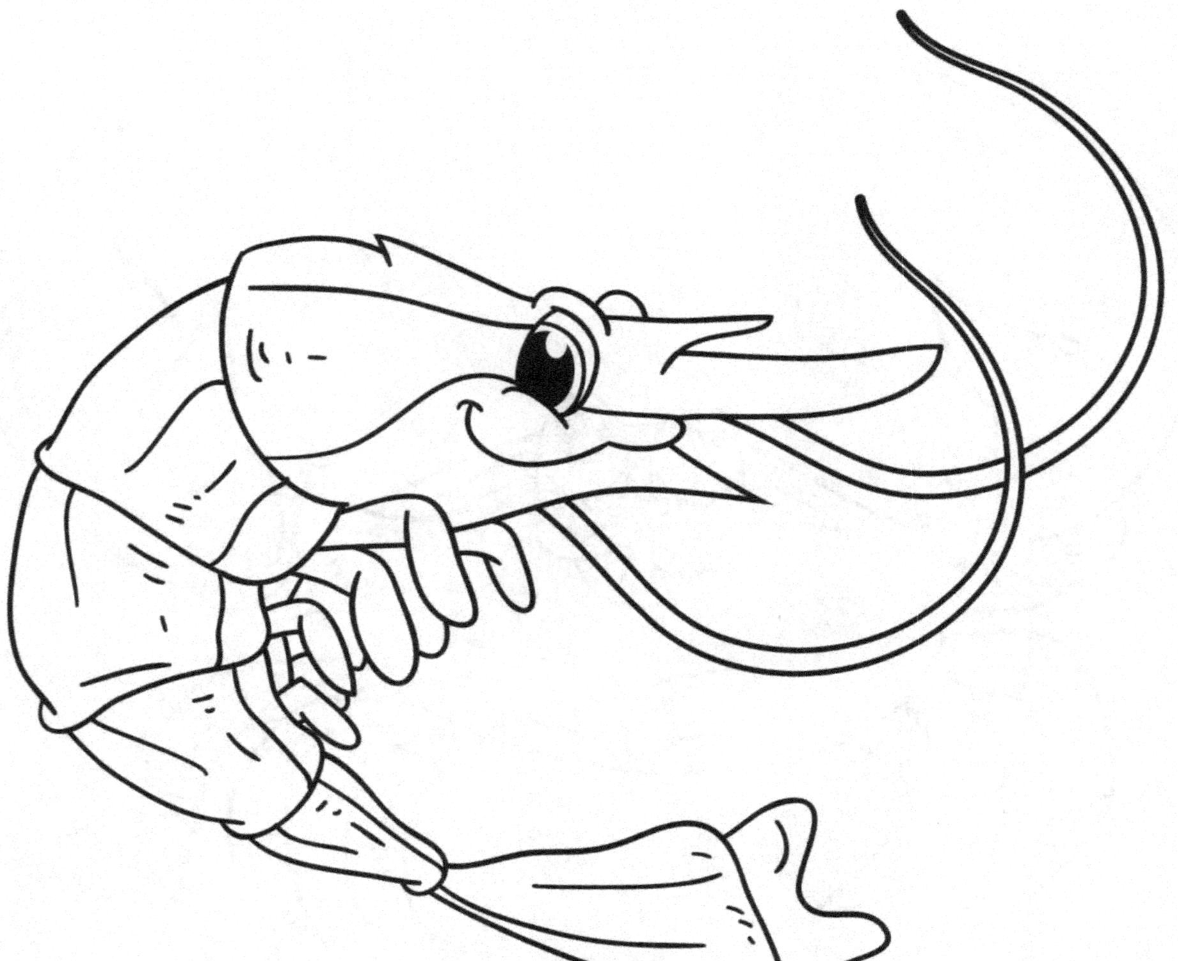

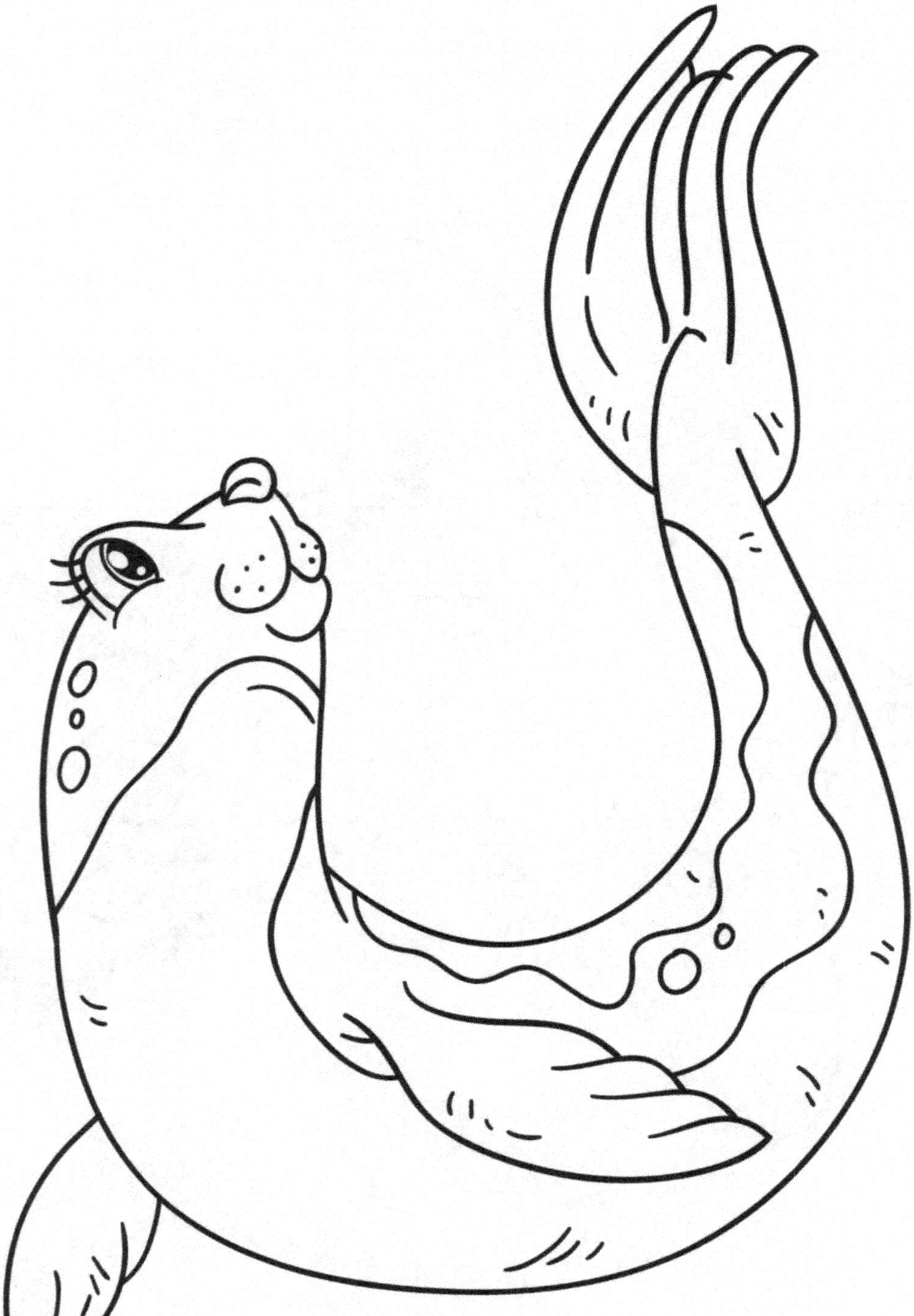

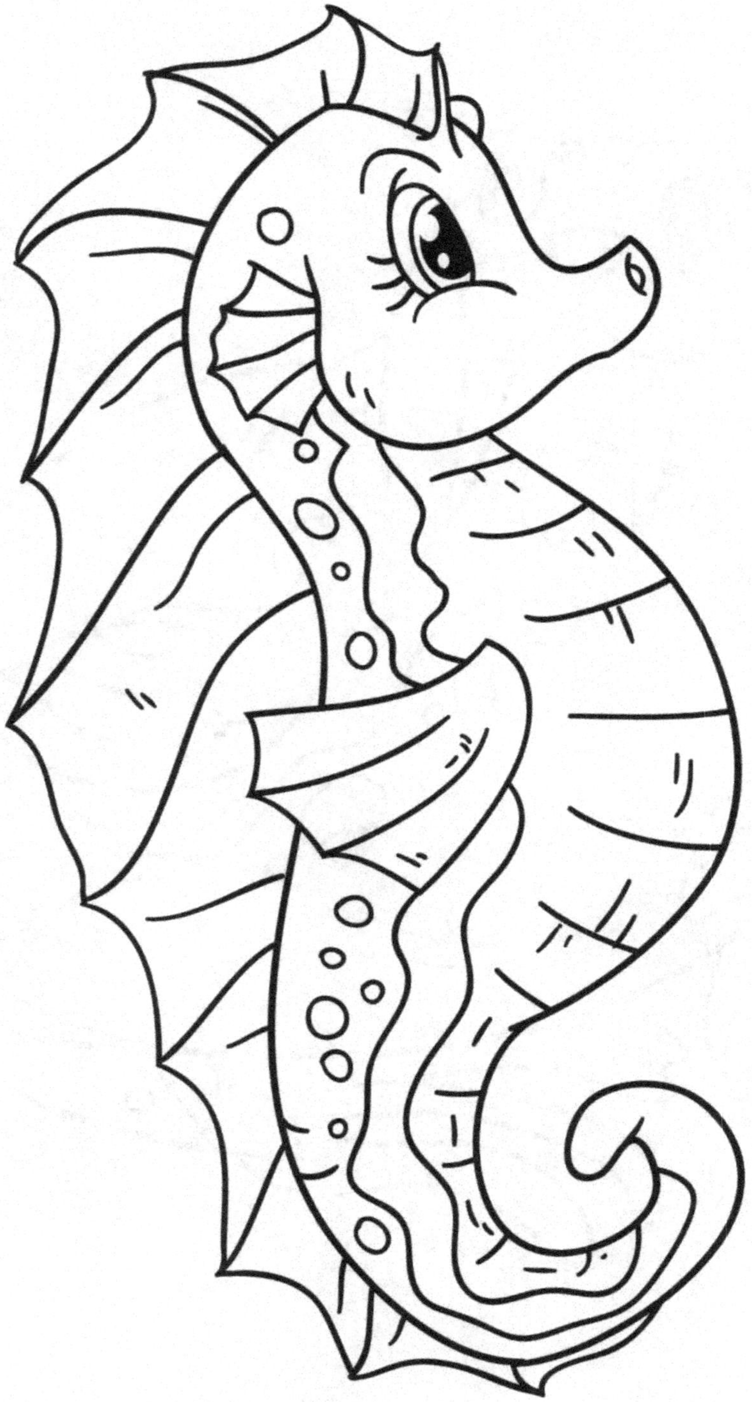

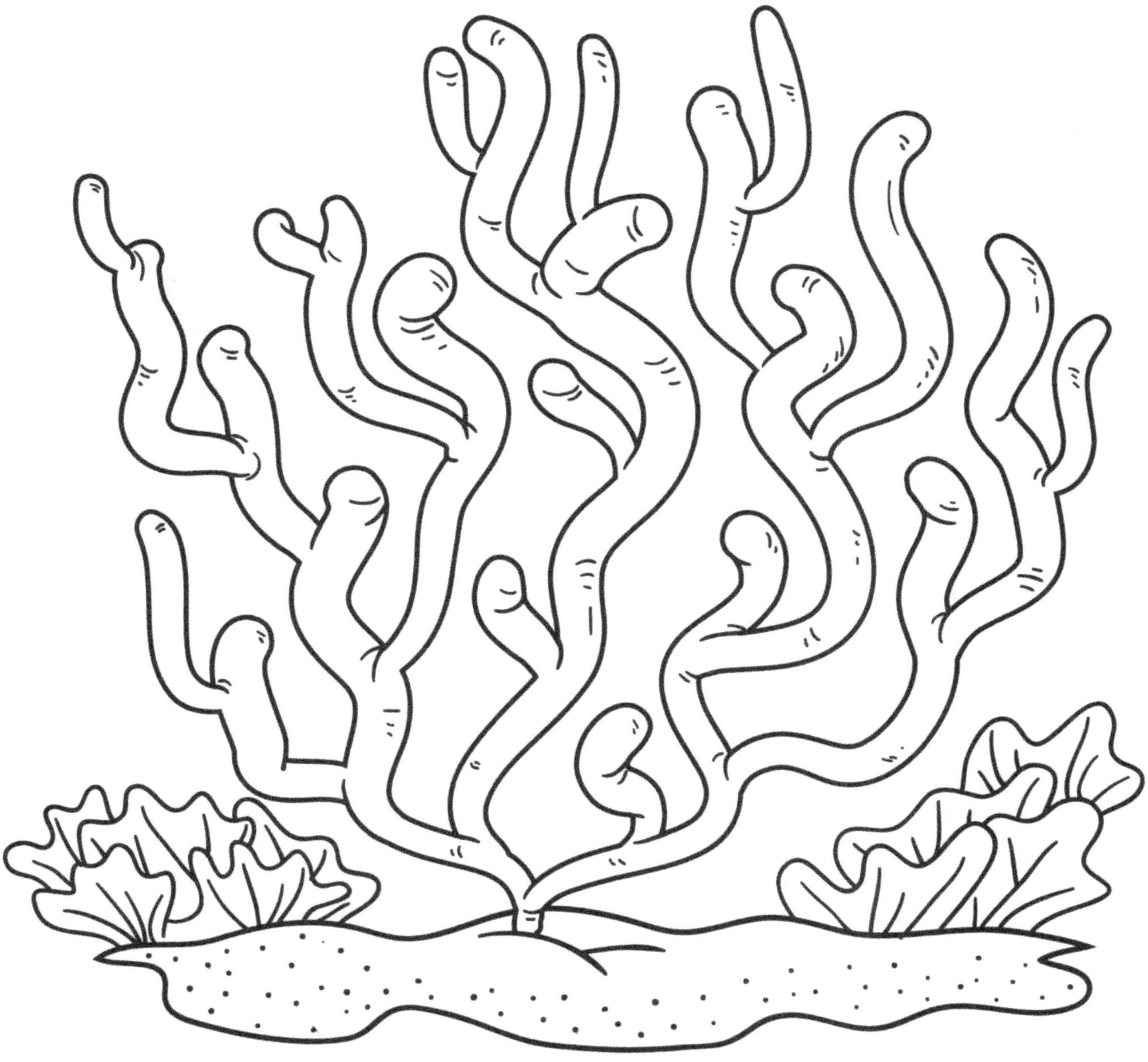

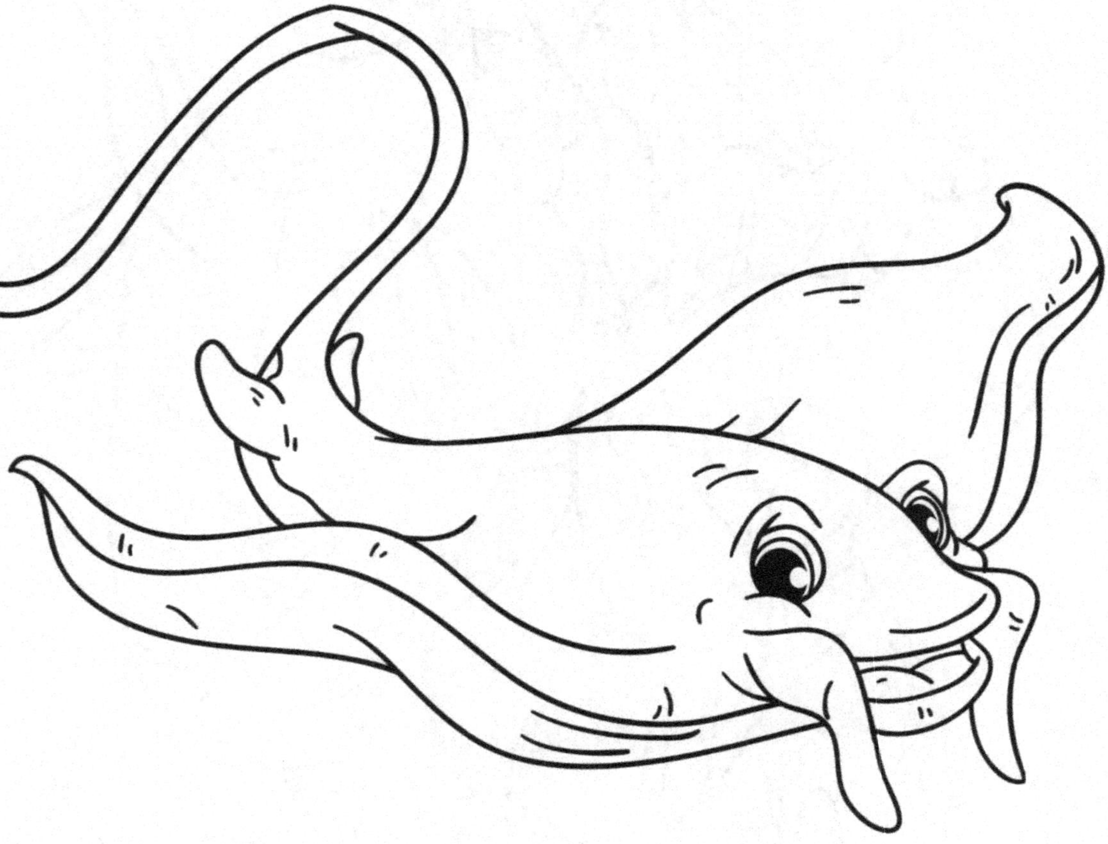

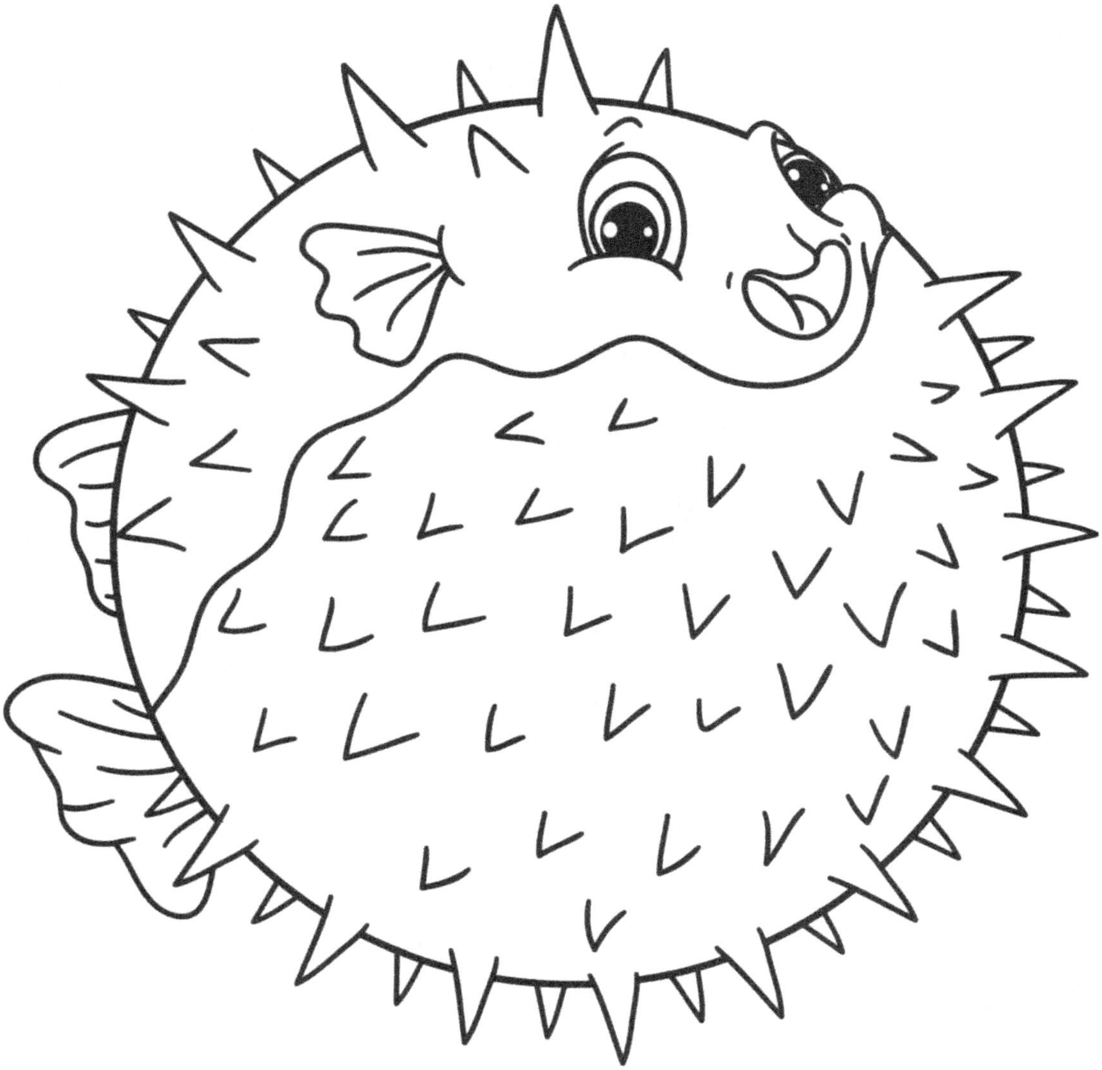

CPSIA information can be obtained
at www.ICGtesting.com
Printed in the USA
LVHW062359230323
742467LV00026B/631

9 781711 053288